# THE SPOILS OF AUGUST

# The Spoils
# of
# August

*by* Barbara L. Greenberg

WESLEYAN UNIVERSITY PRESS

*Middletown, Connecticut*

Acknowledgement is gratefully made to Doubleday and Company and to
Washington Square Press, respectively, the publishers of *Quickly Aging
Here* and *Rising Tides,* two anthologies in which three of the poems in this
book were first published; and to the following periodicals, in the pages
of which a number of other poems in this book were first published: *The
Antioch Review, The Atlantic Monthly, The Beloit Poetry Journal, Epoch,
Falcon, The Michigan Quarterly Review, The Minnesota Review, The New
Republic, Northwest Review, Poetry Northwest, Prairie Schooner, Premiere,
Pyramid, Quartet* and *Shenandoah.*

Library of Congress Cataloging in Publication Data

Greenberg, Barbara L    1932–
      The spoils of August.

      (The Wesleyan poetry program, v. 71)
      Poems.
      I. Title.
      PS3557.R378S6    811'.5'4    73–15012
      ISBN 0–8195–2071–3
      ISBN 0–8195–1071–8 (pbk.)

Manufactured in the United States of America
First edition

# Contents

# THE SPOILS OF AUGUST

## *Admal*

Admal, who was the world
and all the world's belief,
outlived his heartlife. We,

who swore a surgeon's oath
to save him, cut the heart
out of his brother's chest

and sewed it in his own
wherein it fibrillated
twice, then failed. We slew

Annihilus, the son
of Admal, for his proud
young heart. Transplanted, it

beat like a beggar's fist
against an iron door.
Admal rejected it;

rejected, too, the heart
of Serenas, his wife,
and that of Leokin,

brave warrior. There came
a dwarf whose saintmark glowed
bright on his cheek. We seized

his heart and grafted it
in Admal's mediastinum
where it blanched and shrank.

We stuck a pig. Its fat
red heart was bulging as
the sixth incision split

the breast of Admal. Loud,
hard, hot, the pig's heart pumped
like the Avenger's dragon

caged in bone, and broke
the ribs of Admal, who
was all the world. Holy

is the corpse of Admal
and holy is the pig's heart
which rejected him.

## Agnes and Nathaniel, Old

The bony wit of the woman and her frigid nostrils.
And the spiderveins of her husband, blushing beneath his beard.

And the ribcage of the woman. White on X-ray.
Under her phantom breast. Lungpinching fingers.

And the grotto of the man. The sponge he breaths with.
In. And out. Like gums against the nipple.

And the woman's spine. A flute to taunt the flautist.
Her husband's hands. And flowerprints on windows.


The woman crawls on the beach
invading oysters
measuring pearls and piercing
and stringing the pearls on her nerves.

And the man keeps birds in his breast cage
and the birds are singing.
*Never free us, never give us freedom*
say the caged birds.

# Anne, The Purification of

*Take Someone With You.*
*Take a Jew to Church.*

She took a blind boy to the bowling alley.
Pins went down
like chunks of organ music
timbering.

She took a deaf mute to the family sing.

She walked in duty through a storm
holding an umbrella for
a multiple-sclerotic girl
whose skirt and faculties were blown
by a rapist wind.


She fed her plasma
pint by spasm
to the mental hospital

danced on her knees
at the paraplegic's ball

and took a quadruple amputee
home to her bed and spread herself
and let him
like a porcupine.

She chose a killer.
She confessed his crime.

The morning of the guillotine

she willed away
her organs and her tense black hair
whereby her kidneys would survive her deeds
and that thick wig
on some bald stranger's head
outlive her follicles.

And sat upright in bed
forgiving
everything.

## April Thirty-first

And call it the maiden ladies' day.
With lavender water, with attar of roses
flutter them out of their Back Bay houses
out of their West End pots of flowers
out of their North End east wind closets;
ruffle them out of their cotes as pigeons
flush and feather, the maiden ladies
under the sun their silken dresses
kiss kiss kiss in a ringworm pattern.

And summon the beautiful blue police
with blown-up butterfly nets to gather
all the drunks in the Boston Common
swoop and capture, swoop and capture
Billy-the-Bum, sweet William fallen;
raise them, shave them, all in satin
dress them just for the day and dance them
down down down to the Public Gardens
arm in arm with the maiden ladies.

In and out in the Public Gardens
swan by swimming by duck by tree
by bridge and river and flowered path
they'll dance, the maidens, the maiden ladies
sweet and sweaty, the red-nosed rummies
ringing their buttocks above their thighs
like wedding bells. Come down to see.
Come down to see and pack a lunch
and nobody laugh and nobody laugh.

## As a Good Man

I see you as a good man walking inside a pack of dogs.
In willing witness of your perpetual beginnings
I know you now as a good man, keeper of his own kennel.

The dogs are familiar with you, they are all tongue;
they lick your face, paw moistly toward your heart.
You let them love you through their sickly teeth.

And when they sharpen on your bones, you let them.
The yelps, the growls, the wet breath on your groin,
the vermin on your trouser legs. You let them.

Like butcher's meat you acquiesce — and grinning
you let them game you into bloody dog adventures
and hound you through the labyrinths of your kennel.

But tell me again, tell me and I will try to believe you,
how on some windy mornings with the pack behind you,
through miles of open meadow . . . Yourself. You, leading.

## August 27, 1971

1.   they are small they are fat there are many of them
you can touch them they can touch you

they are death

all your life you have been speaking about death
as if you had nothing better
to do with your mouth
than speak about that
thinking death was what would happen once to anyone but

they are small they are ripe they are mad about you
you can squeeze them they are in-
destruct-
ably soft
tomatoes
beginning
to be rancid
like your own
soft
underarms

they have faces
they have eloquent faces
when you step on their faces they cry out
they cry out EEYOW YOU ARE HURTING US BADLY
as if you had hurt them

there are many of them
in the gut in the hair at the root of the tongue
in the rain in the moon in the dust of the parking lot crying

WE ARE YOUR BABIES AND WHY
WERE WE DUMPED FROM THE FREIGHT TRAIN

WE ARE YOUR FINGERS REMEMBER
YOU PROMISED YOU PROMISED

2.   today is your birthday
     (good morning good morning)
     the guests are arriving
     you never invited

     arriving like hemorrhoids
     you never invited
     but daily created
     (the rubbing the rubbing)

     like bullets arriving
     the better to eat you
     (delicious delicious)
     your sin and your virtue

     the better to know you
     they drink from your blisters
     (l'chaim l'chaim)
     they blow out your wishes

     their gift is the mortgage
     you snatch from their fingers
     (oh shylocks sweet shylocks)
     they lend you your life

## Back

Damn you, Gretel, can't you remember
what happened to the bread crumbs? Birds ate them,
beaked them in the air before they fell.
So much for all your why-nots and forevers.
None of it's there. I mean, the story's over,
the legend's written out, and Gretel,
nobody ought to know what happens after.

But if we went, and if we met the neighbors,
and named our names, the old woodcutter's children,
who could convince them that it isn't incest?
Dreams and identities, we lose the details.
Could either of us, Gretel, answer truly
which of us was first and which the foundling?
Yet in the story there's a prince for you.
They'll think of that.

No matter? Then consider,
forgetting the disgrace and disenchantment,
that if a path were cut
through the old woods and the danger
to bring us hand in hand to the old clearing,
Gretel, I swear it, there is no house standing;
but if there is, it is a house of wood;
and if it is not of wood,
why then, Gretel, then
it is a house of sugar
and hung with a carpet of ants.

# Bird-Feeding

Big stupid bird:
you thought I meant come in.
I meant stay out.
I didn't want
your rough misfeathered presence
in my living room.
I should have shut
the window on your crooked feet.

I know it's winter but
why pick on me? I mean,
I hardly know you. You
come flapping in, come croaking
help help help, you spill
your tropicals all over, you
corrupt my thought
You do me damage
with your grateful beak.

I mean, why take
your nervous breakdown
on *my* windowseat
when all I did
was hang the bellseed out?

## Boarding of Pan American Flight 207
## Will Be Delayed Ten Minutes . . .

These are an airport's bones: the pairs of lovers
reopening and closing their embraces
like shellfish breathing, and the knots of children,
anxieties and parents at the parting
of now from ever. We consult our watches.
There are people weeping under the Pan Am sign

and at the insurance kiosk. Shall we sign
for flight insurance, we who are clock-bound lovers
of life, this life, still ticking in our watches
and in our ribs and through our hard embraces?
Or would we crash in vain? This little parting
pinches us with omens and the children

have radar in their minds. We are all children,
leaning toward the tower for a sign,
a wink, a warning. What? Are the clouds parting?
Is the sea? Will lightning part the lovers
and solder strangers into weird embraces?
Each eyes another. Each stranger watches

through shadowed eyes, his shadow. A skyhop watches
baggage carts. A mother counts her children.
Nuns watch each other, but a priest embraces
the host of us and grandly makes the sign
of Christendom, to wave before the lovers.
"And where is the such sweet sorrow in this parting?"

a coed quibbles as the time of parting
is endlessly postponed and we rewind our watches.
. . . *will be delayed ten minutes.* Yet the lovers,

self-winding in their passions, are like children
who will not mind the clock or any sign
except the metric of their own embraces.

. . . *will be delayed ten minutes.* These embraces
define our limbo at the edge of parting
ten minutes deathward. Under the Pan Am sign
we wave good-bye for anyone who watches
and then become each other: parents, children,
friends and rivals, locked in the arms of lovers.

We peep between embraces. Through midnight watches,
our dry lips parting, we prepare the children
for a sign of consummation in these lovers.

## Chambermaid

In this hotel
there's one fine room
that's never entered
on the register.
I clean it

early every morning,
touching the silk,
rubbing the air
until it shines
like glass;

then lock the door.
If there's a guest
he's never there
when I am, but
each morning

there are things
and signs: sheets
a tangle of loving,
fluffs of bad breath
in corners

and God knows what
burnt weightless
in the ashtrays.
I wipe away
a message

soaped on the mirror.
I erase the bed;
I rub the air
until it shines
like glass.

## The Children

The innocent children are marching.
They parade in remarkable numbers.
We stand in our doorways to watch them.

The children are marching and marching.
They have massed on the superhighway.
The traffic is helpless against them.

The children are cross; they are hungry.
They have lost or forgotten their manners.
They gobble the food that they plunder.

Take care: the children are marching.
They have soiled their hands and their faces.
They are bad. They are playing with matches.

What can we do? They are children.
We must send them to bed without supper.
Then we must plan to forgive them.

But the children are marching against us.
They are mad. They are burning our bankbooks.
Now they are storming the armory.

Nothing is safe from the children.
They have fouled our kitchens with excrement.
They are smearing our Bibles.

What swine has perverted the children?
They are lewd. They are plucking their mothers.
They swear to dismember their fathers.

The children. Their conscience is granite.
They deny us a chance to surrender.
They laugh as they stamp on our faces.

We must think. We must think of the past.
We must think of the future.
We must rise and destroy the children.

## Cotillion

It clings to me
like static electricity

this skin-tight dress
this death wish

this knit desire.
I have nothing new to wear.

I had nothing new last year
and the years before

but wore an identical dress
and waltzed with suicide and praised his manliness.

I am not a natural dancer.
I abuse my partner

false step by step
my false mouth at his neck

active with promises.
"Come with me now," he says.

"Later," I cry
and run away

and fondle other lives
between the fingers of my long black gloves

and therefore take my life
without relief

but inch by inch
safe from experience.

# The Deeps

'Do you live on the surface, Aunt Matty?' asked Aubrey.
'No, dear. I? No, I am a person who lives rather in
the deeps, I am afraid.' — Ivy Compton-Burnett

## 1.

I, too, my dears. So many fathoms down
and deep deep deep but never deep enough
to pop a lung and make an end of it.
Think of an ocean bottom ripe with toys
and pearls and fruit and motherlove, and you
withheld above it on a rope of breath
one gasp away. Here in the deeps, my dears,
the muse delivers in a foreign tongue
you never learned at school. A priestly rite
ends as you reach the gate. A peacock fan
unfolds an inch beyond your vision like
the twenty-twenty line you couldn't answer
for the ophthalmologist. Love's mermaid sits
inside the bubble of a sonic boom
and sings the song you'll never hear her singing.
I see my book. It's open to the page
of truth. It lies among the bones. My mind
is catapulting toward it but the fish
have intercepted swift on silver fins
and not a word will go uneaten by them.
I do not curse the fish. I curse my soul,
the limit of its leash, no freer than
a pet chameleon pinned to a boy's lapel.

2.

"Don't float away," his mother said.
That Willie. What a scamp. He did.

He went on waterwings away
with such outlandish buoyancy

that all the mothers in the surf
could not prevent his floating off.

Outlandish boy. He rode the sea
the way a seraph rides the sky

as if he'd learned in utero
that floating free is good to do.

And floated free. And kept his drift
between the flotsam and the fish

across the ocean free and clear
until he reached its navel, where

a dragonfly with dainty fangs
alit and pricked his waterwings.

Then Willynill a bag of bone
unwaterwinged he drifted down

past sharks and squids and submarines
past frogmen and leviathans

to where I waited in the gloom
my pockets full of bubblegum.

How did I love him? More than life
and meant to keep him near and safe

but when I tried to warm his blood
his body broke like moistened bread.

## For David, after His Nightmare

David, I swear it, we are all haunted,
and almost mad, or think we are, or will be.
Even the soldier sleeps with his hand
in his crotch, and the doctor
sweats at the sight of a cat
for an old reason. Even the President
cries in the night for his mother
and frightens the White House.
Night time, some of the time, or almost always
we share ourselves with demons—I can prove it
with facts from an official human census.
I tell you, child, you will never meet
man or woman who has not been, as you are,
afraid to go to sleep or wake up after
or face a wall of darkness or a mirror.
I know your ghosts. They'll ride you like a train
through all your years and all the worlds you're in
and that's a law—so how am I to blame?
I love you better for the dreams you dream.

## The Game of Animals

My pinball game. The game of animals.
My dime. I introduce the ball. I work
the double flipper buttons. I elect-
rify the board; I press; perspire; react-
ivate the bells, the bumper lights, the beasts
from A to Z, from Ape to Zebra, Ark
to Zoo and
          BONUS SPECIAL SUPERBONUS
CHOICE AND SUPERCHOICE!
                        A tilt? No tilt,
but on the board an automatic monkey
grinding his little organ for a winner.
One free replay. A dozen free replays.
A hundred—no, a hundred thousand replays!
My lucky night
          and wait:
                    tomorrow morning
I'll see my children shed their imperfections;
and tattered edges of my life will be
bound up in gold; and nothing in the world
will die of hunger; and there'll be no war.

31

## The Gentleman's Garden

The gentleman's garden
is held secure
>> by a green electric hedge.
Not even a cat
can cheat the hedge
>> whose eye admits no evil.

The gentleman's children
are dumpling good
>> and will not touch the hedge.
Among their mother's
roses they play.
>> They pluck their mother's roses.

Their father whispers
against their cheeks
>> *Good-bye.* His beard is bread.
His children play.
The woman they hear
>> beyond the green hedge, screaming

*My hair is on fire,*
*my face is on fire,*
>> is nothing, is no one they know.
Their father is gentle.
He would not murder
>> something they could not eat.

## Hetty's Solitaire

No and again no says the stubborn deck
and no no no no says
the eternal kibbitzer
above her shoulder where she flings the salt.
Would she ride to debtor's prison
in a chariot?
No says her brother
plucking his long moustache.

Poor Hetty Pityboo, poor Hetty Pet,
with all her little children born and gone
into their father's pocket
and no lover left
to raise a hand against
these fifty-two old enemies.
Poor skinny Henrietta facing death
like one more faded face card with a bent corner.

One after one
the way her chances went
she lays them out — all out — and calmly spits
her lungs out at their pock-marked surfaces:
one after one, by fours,
in thirteen pews
on the cold wood kitchen table
in celebration of her pauper's funeral.

## The Husband

He'd never wrung
the neck of a rabbit
a goose or a sparrow
not any until
in the night
with a cat
at the back of the cellar
he strangled and strangled.

*But why?* said his wife
with the chill on her nipples
and fur in her mouth
and the cat eyes staring.
*Why did you bring it, why bring it to me?*

And the thousands of cats
were the jaws of her question,
they mewed up the night
from their thousands of fences.

He sucked at his tongue and was drunk on the juices.

# I Was Looking

through a crevice at the hunger children
when my hands
dropped from my wrists.

I was looking at the hunger children feeding
on a squirrel's bones
when both my hands, my gentle hands, my dear
caressing doves
fell down.

I was wearing gloves.
I was looking at the hunger children
chewing on their mothers' thighs.
Two-button kidskins and the children's mouths
engaged in mother eating
when my hands
dropped to my lap
and twitched like just dead lobsters. I was

looking. I was thinking
oranges and apples when
my hands in rich white kidskin gloves
the elegant postbellum length
detached like milktree pods and I

was blowing kisses on my severed hands,
my creamy sausages, my once
warm touch knots
when the children bit

the wormy center of their appetites
dying like children in a photograph
which, rubbing lotion
on my stump ends,
I was looking at.

## Impossible Love Song

Young girls like me are always skipping rainbow
while knights like you rush by on black umbrellas.

Old men like you, the emperors of wheelchair,
grope in their laps for young girls skipping rainbow.

There is always someone waiting at a restaurant
for one who should have come but is not born yet;

always a mother clinging to an infant
that rolls uphill, upmountain into manhood.

Women like me are always folding omelets
for suicides who don't come down to breakfast

and boys like you, the hope of sleepless virgins,
lie sound asleep, their arms around each other.

Like you, like me, the poet fills his sonnet
with thirteen lines of grief and one of silence.

This is a hopeless love, star-crossed and thwarted.
If I were not a cynic I would cry my heart out.

## In a Sack of Paradox

I make myself an honest liar saying
*All I say is false.*

I fix my wit
to spy on love and sleep
then loveless sleepless witless
take the doublecross.

Crossing a sea
by mathematical halves I reach
an actual harbor
never.

Let's say my luck
is gagged bound locked in an abandoned car
on a dark dirt road in gangland.

*We'll come and get you*
*when you don't expect it*
said the hatchetman.
That's why I wake
each morning asking
*Now? This afternoon? Tonight?*
with expectation dangling like a noose.

I hold my breath.
I swear to stop the intake
once and forever but the idiot brain
gets motherly and opens up my lungs.

*What does it feel like to be really dead?*
I ask a dead man and he winks at me.

## J. P. in the Surf

As if the waves were dragon paws
they slap his corpulence, they pound
—better than Swedish hands—his lard
to dolphin sleekness and the most
brave body in the sea is his. Not
the boys in wanton beer games but
Sir J. P. Dragonfedder rides
the biggest wave its climax in
over the tops of everyone. And
red silk swim-trunks on his rump
say J. P. Hero while the tails
of dragonkind flap back applause
big, bigger, beyond all shores as

J. P. Puddle bestrides the beach,
blankets beside his wife and strokes
—deeper than any flesh—the sand
as if the sand were money.

# Just After the Widow's Death

1. *The Living Room*

Her Chinese lamps
are finished sentences
and her philosophies
are hammered silver snakes with ruby eyeballs.
At her hearth
are once-upon-a-childhood wishes made and granted.

On every wall of this, her ceremonial room,
are clear glass shelves
(like sleeping water or we know not what
pure stratum of her completed self)
where round jewels balance.

Her poet, bound in leather, suffers
no misinterpretation.
Twin porcelain angels in a blush of health
repeat her prayers
and three jade dragons
like contented appetites
forget how fierce their purpose.
On the mantlepiece a crystal bird
sings winter light and consummated loves.

## 2. *The Bedroom*

What dime store stylist has . . . ? I mean
the flapping ruffles, the embarrassments of dust,
the goldfish bubbling in their . . . No,
not plaster spaniels, not

the hot pink palsy of her . . . Oh, but yes,
it is. Her pink, her bed, her flowered wall,
her Saint Cecilia framed in tin, her box
of, in their fluted nests, soft center chocolates
each bitten into . . .

There is no message
scotch-taped to the mirror, reading
"Friends, remember . . . "

What is is twisted on the bed:
a wash-gray sleepy doll, its button eyes
torn off, its once-enamelled mouth
a crusty streak, an insolent cry of
*want, I want, I want.*

## Lines from a Caribbean Balcony

I mean to say, the scenery is mine.
The balcony. The sugarbirds. The shell.
Also the sea that says the things I mean.

I plant the birds. They bloom in jessamine,
mimosa, bougainvillaea, asphodel . . .
I mean to say, the scenery is mine.

The conch is also mine. I let it moan
into my ear, a skull against my skull.
It quotes the sea and says the things I mean.

*All's well,* it says. *Fear nothing but the moon.*
*No ships go down; no swimmers call for help.*
I call the birds. The scenery is mine.

And when the waves break with the bones of men
I break the blue-green motion of myself
to praise the sea, which says the things I mean.

*All's well,* I say. The small birds say *amen.*
*There are no meanings,* says the empty shell.
I mean to say, the scenery is mine.
I teach the sea to say the things I mean.

# The Middleman

I'm Laban Gross, the salesman for
K'dosh Memorial Gardens. I'm
a friend you haven't met yet. Wait.
Some night when you're in bed asleep
or making love, I'll ring you up.
I've got your private number. Private
is my cup of tea. I've got
a lot of plots. For you I've got
a custom built forget-you-not
to buy on time, to plant you in
in 5, 10, 50 years — who's counting?

Pick up the phone. *Shalom, I say.*
*Shalom. How goes it, friend? Not good?*
*Forgive the hour, not wanting to be*
*interrupting something  Nothing?*
*So call me names. It's not the sweep*
*who makes the soot — you get my meaning?*
*And Rabbi Eliezar says*
*you plan ahead, you sleep much better.*
*Please. Forgive a fellow man*
*a little joke. You want instead*
*that I should say how young you're getting?*

*Not yet,* you say. That's good. By me
that's fine, I want to try again
tomorrow and tomorrow. Soon
you'll know me better, call me Laban,
tell me dirty stories, feel
sorry for me yet, like maybe
I'm your brother Cain. And soon

you wouldn't dare to shut your eyes
until I call to chew the fat
and push a plot and let you know
I count you still among the living.

## Mom Cries, Python Dies

—UPI news story

Like Mrs. R. Rivera
of the Philippines
who screamed before
she fainted, I
beheld the python
coiled in the crib
about to eat my infant.
I saw the hard
slow muscle of its head
and saw its eyes
fixed on my son asleep
and saw its dark
extravagant length
looped on the mattress
like an abandoned
garden hose. I saw
a tattooed organ
giving birth. I saw
my father's penis
smiling and my mother's
teeth. And the long tongue
of the past stretched out
to bind me in that myth
which is continually
swallowing. At which I
screamed. To which six men
replied with knives
and killed the serpent
and my son was spared

as we must all be
spared. *Father-in-heaven,*
*let us dream our lives*
*in secret. Protect us from*
*our snakes, oh hide them*
*in the tall grasses*
*far from our habitation.*
*And visit not our sins*
*on Mrs. R. Rivera*
*of the Philippines.*

## Mother, R. I. P.

When our dead mother came back on the tenth
anniversary of her death, wearing
a floor-length flowered shift with a straw hat
over the wiglet and the bottled tan,
we all assured her that she hadn't aged
a day, that she had lost some weight, that she
had gained a worldliness which often comes
with travel. What we felt in secret was
how smug she seemed, considering the tears
we'd spent on her behalf and all those mums
we'd planted at her grave. She poured the tea
like Lady Astor at the Orphan's Home
— *Another lump of sugar dear?* — while we,
wanting to squeeze her hand, wanting to sing
or rage, wanting to tell her every day's
adventures, every year's meanderings,
sat at her feet like stone. Said nothing true.
Said *Bless you mother* when she stood to leave
and never learned, and never thought to ask,
where she had been, what she was heading toward.

## Nancy in Love with War

Nancy
in love with war
is swinging
in the bombed out building
from the one surviving
chandelier
> UP
> GOES
> HER
pinafore
her ruffle wings
her legs a V for

Fields of wheat and Nancy Nancy
bone white    blood red    pure as folksong
singing for the bold the soldiers
Nancy their dear their darling

At the harbor / at the shelter / at the Grand Hotel /
at the clinic / at the tavern / at the refugee asylum /
at the market / at the dance hall / at the orphans' home /
or down at the depot a basket of grapes on her arm
> *Father have you seen her*
> *have you seen our Nancy?*

Dipping her hands in their wounds    her hands
shine with their blood    her fingers
pinch their shattered valves    her tongue
throbs in their bulletholes    her breath
is in their lungs    their breath
she wraps them in her shawl

Who has known the widow Nancy?
The generals have known her.
They rape her on the battleground
while bullets graze their buttocks.
The corpses, too, have known her.
They fasten on her nipples.
She pumps them full of glory.
She denies them nothing.

She is a woman whose name is Nancy who is in love with war
which is her enemy. Obscene positions she assumes to please him
please him for a moment only. His demands upon her quicken
as she ages. As she falters he invents new exercises for her.
As she pleads for satisfaction he invades her children saying:
> *Put on a black dress, harlot.*
> *Gather for their graves wildflowers.*

## Old Men Die Old

Old men talk to old men;
they are almost deaf.
Their words sound back at them
from some cold place.
They cannot rid themselves
of what they speak
or the perpetual taste of ashes
in their acrylic teeth.

Virginia cares for an old man
and rubs his skin:
the loose skin of his cheeks
and of his testicles,
and the parched skin of his lower back,
a thin suede,
and the cobwebbed hammock of his abdomen.

Granduncle tastes the wine.
The wine is good.
Dry, not overdry. Mature.
Big-nosed and with an honest bite
and much my kind of wine
granduncle says
to the Elizabeth who brings the cup
and then the napkin to granduncle's lips.

At last night's wedding banquet
there was one who danced
much more than any other guest.
The bride, the white swan, filled his arms
waltz after waltz
while all the company looked on
astonished and the groom rejoiced
to see the old man lasting
like a deity.

## Omegas

### 1.

Killing the defective
infant is not necessarily
more difficult than
giving birth to it.
You select a feather
pillow. You apply it
to the countenance.
You resist the argument
of quaint and muffled
voices in your fingertips.
You ignore the innocent
motion of the arms and legs
if, in the case of
your particular infant,
these exist. You must
bear down. You must permit
three hundred seconds
to escape before you can
complete the accident
and be relieved of it.

### 2.

You and your innocent
are lying in the sun and she
is teaching you the language of
defective children.
You can trace
the hieroglyphics of her spinal cord
and fix them into words:

a word for *warmth*
a word for *breathing-in-and-out*
another word for *silence*
and a word for *face*.
Your child's tongue is clotted
and she has no eyes.

3.

God will bear down on your head
with a cloud
shaped like a pillow.
You will catch a glimpse of His dramatic nostrils
before your eyes are cancelled
in His alphadome.
You will not lie still.
Your quaint defective body will contend
against His murdering.
With all your clotted language you will sing to Him.

## Personae Displaced

We are scribbled in pencil on foolscap.
Our lives have no meaning.
A chapter of song is no truer to us
than a chapter of digging.

One page of our life is too many
and a thousand are insufficient
for we die and have never stopped dying
yet reach no conclusion.

Our tongues are like cactus leaves.
What voice shall we use?
We have lost the particular language
of our fathers' gravestones.

Our stars have no names.
We are ruled by the burden of morning.
Our thoughts are a compost to shovel and spread
on the weeds in our garden.

Our salt has no taste.
Our tears are as daily as urine.
Our blood is the verdict of rust on our bones.
We have no reasons.

## 2

Sudden they come and clean, of clean complexion.
Out of their bindings they come, gilt-edged and deckled.

Onto our beds they climb, and sigh, and couple
into a throb of love beyond instruction.

Even our bedding shines with moonlit honey.
Even our air is blessed, transfused with incense.

Out of our wooden arms they lift our children
promising words and worlds we never dreamed of.

Onto our windowpane they splash a landscape.
Out of our piano they bring incredible music;

out of our well, sweet water; out of our soil,
grapes and roses; out of our granite, gems.

Out of the cupboard where our breadcrumbs molder
they have reaped abundance, spread a feast where

suddenly damask, crystal, candles; suddenly
wine; suddenly meat and fruit and pastry;

suddenly in our lives a banquet table
steaming with life, to which we are not invited.

3.

Treasures we never knew we owned
were stolen from us.
We have met the thieves.

We have seen our names imprinted
on a list of victims
boldface italic in the evening papers.

Ten new commandments
have been delivered with the late editions;
ten thousand soldiers

but the thieves are dauntless.
They die and become immortal
which they will not teach us.

When they come tomorrow
bearing lighted torches
we will greet them, crying:

*Burn us.*
*We are crudely written.*
*We were meant to burn.*

# Pinchmouth

Pinchmouth is weaving hairs.
That arthritic spider
holding tweezers is the
hand of Pinchmouth weaving
human hair, creating

fabric out of blond, brown,
red, black, gray, whatever
friendship offers. "I have
many friends," says Pinchmouth.
"Show me one," says Wiggins.

"Many friends," says Pinchmouth.
"In their graves," says Wiggins.
"Shine your skull," says Pinchmouth
with a spit, despising
old, bald, greasy Wiggins

who collects the barber's
sweepings and the refuse
from the public sinkbowl.
Wiggins would scalp a corpse.
Not Pinchmouth. All *his* hairs

are friendship pluckings. He
remembers names. He thinks
of wet hair, windblown hair,
love locks on pillows. He
is old, sick, going blind

but weaving everyone
together—everyone
except for Wiggins who
is old, sick, going blind,
bald as a roach, worthless.

## Poem for a Dead Aunt

I dream you naked on a float, blown up
enormous and attached to strings
like, in a bright parade, a rubber clown
whose painted membrane might
at any moment in the hot fat sun, explode.
All that trapped air. As if your heart
in a last fit of love let go
a jet of gases and ballooned your skin
ten times beyond its former sense and shape.
Tipped to the sky, your nose, your nipples,
capping the hollow breasts like lewd berets,
and the appalling contour of your belly
that the wind wrinkles . . .

Skipping beside you like a faithful poppet
I blow my message in a paper horn.
*All a mistake* I cry, but nobody listens.
*Terrible error* I tell them. *Cover your eyes
or cover the body over.* Nobody does.
Confetti sprays upon us from dirigibles,
from lungs of fever, and a band brays.
*Cancer* I bellow. *Cancer and the plague!*
and turn against you with a sharp thing in my hand.

## Poem for Susan

After you dived from the barnacled rocks and chilled
        your blood in the ocean
you climbed back up to our summer house, your dark
        hair tangled in the sunset,
and told us about the spinster woman, the maiden
        aunt who lives in you.

You said that nothing you are is yours and nothing
        you do consumes you;
that even when you are most in love, most ardent
        with men or women,
the pitiful spinster pulls at your limbs and blushes
        and burns with envy.

And her eyes behind your eyes, you said, are yellow
        and wet with fever
like fishes' eyes, implacably sad, beyond your power
        to close them.
Even your sleep is not your own. She walks on your
        dreams like a spider.

But when you run with the dogs, dance in a red dress,
        outsing the choir,
you stir and torment the spinster woman, because she
        is always watching,
and you will have no cut flowers in your house, nor
        lace on your dresses, to spite her.

Even your own dear daughters and sons, who touch
        your hair and embrace you,
are quills in her loveless, childless heart. She shivers
        and begs your pardon.

Again you hug your children—again—to feel her
                wince in your being.

This is the photograph we took when you climbed
                the cliff to our cottage:
your features carved by the ocean wind and your hair
                stretched out uncensored
and the spinster woman crouched in the rocks, invisible
                as granite.

## Simpson

Simpson, age fifty, freezes
at the summit of the stairs
perceiving all descent as
perpendicular. "Let's go.
Get moving, Simpson. Take it
one step at a time." Too late.
The downhill muscles falter
and the bones go limp. One foot
fumbles at a wall of glass
while old friends offer crutches.

Simpson forgives the future—
offers to divorce his wife
(once a ballerina, twice
a mother); obliterates
his treasures; tears his clothing;
exposes to his children
a naked Simpson squatting
for his stool. He counts his teeth.
He quotes Ecclesiastes
(weeping) and he quotes himself.

Simpson looks down. A young girl
at the bottom stair looks up,
inhales, is calling *Simpson*
holding out her arms, her hair
like rain, her breasts, her armpits
wet with rainbow and her mouth
like blood. Flamingoes hurry
through the glen. Snakes in their caves
are hissing. A boy on skis
sets out to cross the glacier.

## Sleep Sonnet

The hill is of no color now. The sheep
are flat transparencies. The sheep advance
in tens and hundreds, are absorbed like sleet
into the valley where the carnivores
have cast their shadows. I am not awake.
The hill dissolves in chemicals. The ghost
of no one I remember strokes my face
demanding nothing, and the fleece is soft.
The wolf is not here. It is not his mouth
against my throat. These bloodshot molecules
that circle in the dark are not his eyes
in search of anyone. His appetite
is absent, I can swear to it. The sheets
are white — dead white — and I am not asleep.

*Solitaire*

You play yourself
with pips,
with paper masks.
You learn to lose

as, in a dream,
your own face in a cage,
you thrust your sword
against another face

and your own blood
flows down.
There is a force
that swallows you

inside your mind.
It is a mouth.
It is an answer to
the thousand arguments

you fail to win.
Who wins?
Who holds the sword?
Who moves your thoughts around?

Whose face is that
turned black and blue
behind the King of Clubs?
*Oh there you are!*

## Song for a Daughter

In fields yellow with wheat and birds
I am a young girl and my mother
is a young girl and my mother's
mother multiplied
by all our generations we are
wonderful together
and we are dancing
barefoot in the fields of Canaan
where all their hands
are my hands hot from holding.

The sun is Latvian hot.
The wind fans out from Prussia.
The sky is Babylonian gold.
Our language as we touch and sing is
virgin language understood
like water rushing in our skins
or circles
or the yellow birds
or dancing in these swollen fields
to overtake our mother's promises.

The bearded rabbis
wag their beards
in pleasure
and forsake their scrolls
to fling us kisses from the ghetto walls.

## The Spoils of August

(Gloucester, 1972)

You have slept for a month on the beach;
you are not to be trusted.
The tide that went out with your feces
comes back with your supper
and here is the moon on the water—
a visiting nurse
who opens your navel and fixes
your thumb in your mouth.

You have slept for a month on the beach;
you are not to be trusted.
You will walk in your sleep. You will murder
your favorite uncle
and cover his face with saliva
and swallow his eyes
which are green like your own. You will do it
as fast as a sea-gull.

You have slept for a month on the beach;
you are not to be trusted.
Your lips will be large and your tongue
will be covered with algae.
Attacking the dogs on the beach
you will frighten yourself
with your *ba   ba-ba-ba   ba-ba-ba*
*ba-ba-ba-ba-ba   ba.*

## Survival

If ever I am an old lady
I want to be an elegant old lady
redolent of pungent essences, like bayberry.

I plan to be lean
with Gothic hands and vein-embroidered skin
and prominent eyes that know what most things mean.

My great-granddaughters will be wary
of my eyes, my scent, my strange vocabulary.
I shall serve them tea and wafers while I sip sherry.

I shall make them mine with trinkets:
handkerchiefs and scarabs, wigs and lockets,
skeletons and seashells. I shall fill their baskets.

Then they will ask me for my story
and I shall tell them — tell a phantom story
frail as candleberry smoke. Truer than history.

# 227–2272

This voice is a recording in the wilderness.
The circuits are all in use now. Nevertheless,
thank you for calling Barbara in your hour of stress.

You wish to report disaster at your address?
Fire? Flood? Earthquake? Avalanche? Small craft in distress?
This voice is a recording in the wilderness

and can not reach the Coast Guard. Let this voice express
a sense of deep involvement in your SOS.
Thank you for calling Barbara in your hour of stress.

You wish to report a crime? You wish to confess?
Don't blame yourself. We are all guilty, more or less.
This voice is a recording in the wilderness

and will not reach a verdict. What it says, it says
by careful prearrangement with your consciousness.
Thank you for calling Barbara in your hour of stress.

Hello. Hello.     Are you there? Are you there?  Yes. Yes.
Will you help me? Will you help me?  Godbless. Godbless.
This voice is a recording in the wilderness.
This voice is a recording in the wilderness.

## Two Women

They are walking apart from the children.
*Her* dress and *her* dress are touching.
When they turn to each other to whisper
their cameos meet.

    *Her* whispering voice is a finger
    that slides through the ear of the other.

Two women. Too close to. Together.
The hair on their legs and their forearms.
*Her* breath and the mist on *her* glasses.
Words that they speak.

    *Her* words are as stubborn as honey
    and drool to the mouth of the other.

Too close to. Too slow. But the children
attacking *her* limbs and *her* clothing,
*her* hair and the hoops in *her* earlobes,
have ripped them apart.

    They fall on the grass and are loosened
    and laughing and gleaming with sweat.

## The Victim

A thin wool coat was the jew of him.
Young, he saw it hanging in the attic;
left it hanging, sleeping in the attic;
never let it kiss his back.
Grown, he pawned it,
kept the ticket,
went on eating buttered steak.

At that long table where the guests are faceless
*he* was faceless, chewing on his years,
exhausting through the ciphers of his nostrils
anonymous smoke, like locks of loose gray hair;
and couldn't cry, with nothing to put the tears in
and nothing tragic moving in his veins.
Reflecting on a teaspoon he discovered
his teeth were dead jews' bones.

An awkwardness on Sunday was the jew of him:
a special sense of meat and milk, an eye for noses,
an appetite for fat, a matchstick cross
to crucify a puppet—rot and nonsense.
The jew of him was limp, his life was limp,
a this, a that, a chronic indigestion.
*Oh God, a pill, a tonic.*
                                    In his blood
the desecrated temples burned.

Rain falls on synagogues in Amsterdam.
In Prague. In Athens. In Jerusalem.
Rain falls on synagogues and stains them gray.
Rain in Venice
invokes the odor of canals

where Shylock flesh decays, decays.
He smells it, he
refuses to be disgusted, he
despairs of knowing
what hideous things his own breath might be saying.

A lump of soap is the jew of him.
A yellow band, a hill of bones, a pound of glue.
The thin wool coat a scarecrow wears
warms no one.
He wags on a leash of wind, a tail of wind,
a jew, a jape, a nothing much, an echo.
*Jesus,* he cries, and *Hitler Hitler Hitler*
but not a sparrow answers with his name.

## The Yellowed Woman

The yellowed woman
to whom we bring
our human juices
despises nothing
nor does she love

      anything more
      than anything else.

What we give her
is all she wants
to feed the boil
inside the kettle
the more to stir

      like anyone's mother
      making soup.

And when the sum
of human odor
out of the kettle
clouds her head
what she breathes is

      only another
      kind of air

as night is kind
and makes no choices
or deaf men listen
to answer Yes what-
ever the question.